A New Beginning

CELEBRATING THE SPRING EQUINOX

BY

Wendy Pfeffer

ILLUSTRATED BY

Linda Bleck

DUTTON
CHILDREN'S
BOOKS

DUTTON CHILDREN'S BOOKS
A division of Penguin Young Readers Group
Published by the Penguin Group
Penguin Group (USA) Inc., 375 Hudson Street, New York, New York 10014, U.S.A.
Penguin Group (Canada), 90 Eglinton Avenue East, Suite 700, Toronto, Ontario, Canada M4P 2Y3 (a division of
Pearson Penguin Canada Inc.) · Penguin Books Ltd, 80 Strand, London WC2R 0RL, England · Penguin Ireland, 25 St
Stephen's Green, Dublin 2, Ireland (a division of Penguin Books Ltd) · Penguin Group (Australia), 250 Camberwell Road,
Camberwell, Victoria 3124, Australia (a division of Pearson Australia Group Pty Ltd) · Penguin Books India Pvt Ltd, 11
Community Centre, Panchsheel Park, New Delhi - 110 017, India · Penguin Group (NZ), 67 Apollo Drive, Rosedale, North
Shore 0745, Auckland, New Zealand (a division of Pearson New Zealand Ltd) · Penguin Books (South Africa) (Pty) Ltd, 24
Sturdee Avenue, Rosebank, Johannesburg 2196, South Africa
Penguin Books Ltd, Registered Offices: 80 Strand, London WC2R 0RL, England

Published in the United States by Dutton Children's Books,
a division of Penguin Young Readers Group
345 Hudson Street, New York, New York 10014
www.penguin.com/youngreaders

Designed by Irene Vandervoort

Manufactured in China   First Edition

ISBN 978-0-525-47874-4

1 3 5 7 9 10 8 6 4 2

For Wade, Evan, Margaret, and Miranda
W.P.

For my children, David and Sarah, and my husband, David.
L.B.

Leaf buds uncurl on bare branches.

Frogs leave their winter hideaways,

hop to the nearest water, and lay eggs.

Crocus tips poke through melting snow,

woodchucks whistle, chickadees chirp,

and dragonflies emerge from rivers and ponds.

The long nights of winter shorten,

and with more hours of sunlight,

the weather warms.

In the northern half of the world,

winter gives way to spring.

Robins wing their way back north,
and animals give birth to their young.
People prepare their fields
and plant crops in the softening earth.

As the bright sun returns,

    people open their windows to welcome

    warm breezes and clear out winter's dust.

    We pack away our bulky jackets and wear brightly colored

    clothes to match the fresh shades of spring.

The days gradually grow longer, the nights shorter,

until, around March 21, day and night are equal.

On this day the earth is tilted so that the sun is directly

over the equator.

This day is called the spring *equinox*, meaning *equal night*.

Winter's over, spring begins.

In many cultures' calendars,

the spring equinox marks a new year,

just as January 1 is the beginning of our calendar year.

For thousands of years, in different places and in different

ways, people have celebrated spring as a time of new

beginnings, when the land becomes alive again.

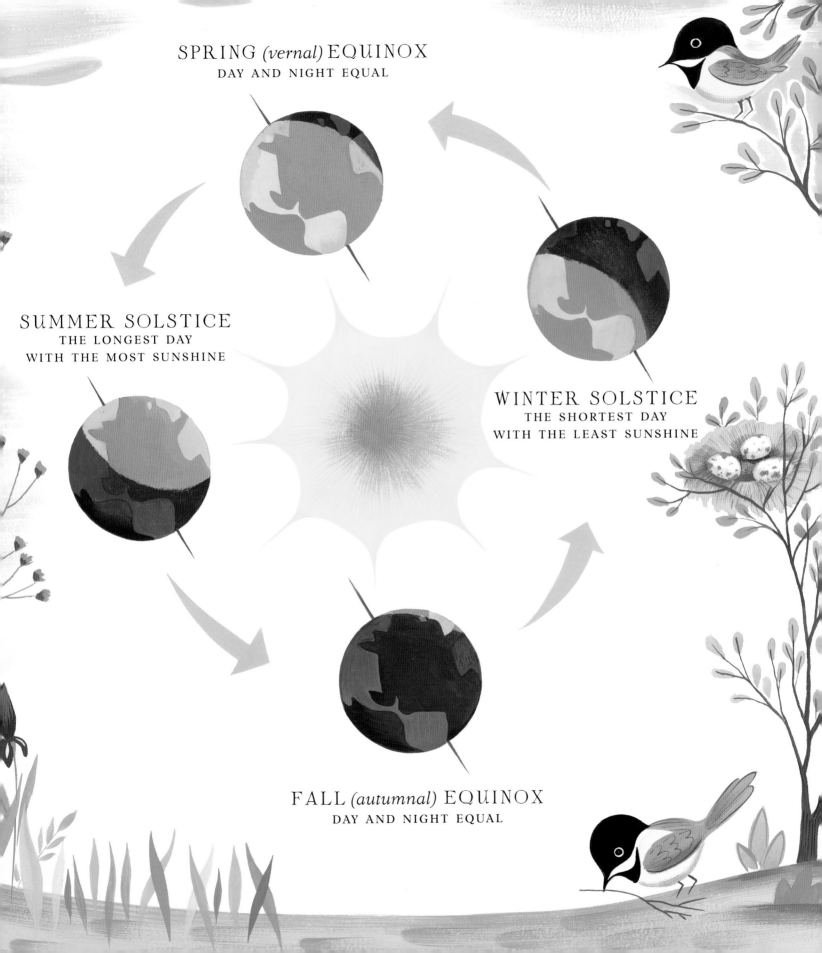

SPRING *(vernal)* EQUINOX
DAY AND NIGHT EQUAL

SUMMER SOLSTICE
THE LONGEST DAY
WITH THE MOST SUNSHINE

WINTER SOLSTICE
THE SHORTEST DAY
WITH THE LEAST SUNSHINE

FALL *(autumnal)* EQUINOX
DAY AND NIGHT EQUAL

Long ago, some say too long to be traced,
the Chinese began celebrating the end of winter
and a new beginning, spring.

Today the second new moon after the winter solstice
still marks the Chinese New Year.

Families clean their homes to sweep away traces of bad luck.

They buy fruits and flowers, hang red banners with
good wishes written on them.

Dancers wear paper lion masks to scare away evil spirits
and bring good luck.

Children receive money in red bags,
since red means good luck, too.

On the fifteenth night, people parade with paper lanterns while fireworks fill the air.

Children cheer as a long silk-and-paper dragon weaves its way down the street to the beat of a drum.

The dragon's appearance is a way of wishing peace, fortune, and good luck to all during the coming year.

Over 3,000 years ago,

the people of ancient Persia celebrated the spring equinox

as a new beginning during No Ruz, which means New Year.

Today, modern-day Iranians welcome spring

just as the ancient Persians did.

Ten days before No Ruz, they plant wheat or barley in a flat dish

to represent new beginnings and the cycle of life.

A few days later,

colorfully dressed troubadours announce

the coming of the New Year.

On No Ruz, families stay home and wait for the exact time

the spring equinox begins.

Many exchange gifts, think good thoughts, do good deeds,

and eat candied fruits to sweeten their lives.

They believe that joy and happiness defeat bad spirits.

Over 2,000 years ago, the people of India celebrated Holi
   at the beginning of spring to ensure good crops.
In Hindu mythology, Holika was a demoness who
   burned in a fire.
Now during Holi on the night of the full moon in March,
   the villagers light giant bonfires to represent the triumph
   of good over evil.
The heat of the bonfire is a sign of the hot summer to come,
   and the villagers bury the ashes to grow better crops.

The next morning, the mood changes from gloomy to jolly.

People of all ages toss multicolored powder with glitter
over each other and load squirt toys with red-tinted
water to spray on anyone passing by.

They all celebrate the coming of spring, singing and dancing,
with soaking-wet rainbow-colored clothes.

Many believe this was the origin of April Fools' Day,
when people play tricks on one another.

About 1,200 years ago, the Maya people in Mexico
built many structures to map the cycles of the sun.
Their existence centered on the sun and its effect
on planting and harvesting.
With their vast knowledge of astronomy, architecture, and
mathematics, the Maya carefully planned and precisely
built structures to predict the seasons.

At Chichen Itza they built the El Castillo pyramid.

Here people can still witness an amazing feat.

Each year on the day of the spring equinox, the afternoon
sun makes shadows that look like the body of a
snake, over 100 feet long, slithering down the pyramid.

At sunset the body joins a huge stone carving of a snake
head, located at the bottom of the main staircase.

Spring has arrived. Planting can begin.

Maslenitsa, or Pancake Week, in Russia dates back
over 1,000 years.

This seven-day sun festival celebrated the returning light.

It bade good-bye to the long winter and hello to spring.

Families ate warm, round, golden pancakes that looked
like the sun.

The more butter they spread on each pancake, the hotter the sun
was supposed to be during the coming summer.

They enjoyed horse-drawn-sleigh rides in a semicircular trail
across the snow, symbolizing the sun's path across the sky.

Today families still celebrate outdoors.

They dance, sing songs, jingle bells,

    enjoy hot tea, and, of course, eat pancakes.

At night bonfires are lit.

Brightly dressed straw scarecrows, representing

    Lady Maslenitsa, are tossed into the fire.

When Maslenitsa is over, spring begins.

Almost 500 years ago, when the Cree Native Americans experienced long, hungry winters, berries, one of the first signs of spring, were an important sign of the warm season to come.

They not only ate the berries, but because bears feasted on them, too, the Cree knew where to hunt bears.

They honored the first berries each year by placing them in a bowl, holding them high, and thanking the Great Spirit.

The Jewish holiday of Passover celebrates a new beginning.

Over 3,000 years ago, Hebrews were slaves in Egypt.

After 400 years of slavery, they were finally freed.

Each spring, on the first night of the eight-day holiday,
     families gather for a meal called a seder.

They eat special foods, sing songs, and retell the story of
     how they became free.

Each food on the seder plate tells a different part of the story.

A lamb bone symbolizes the lamb that was sacrificed
in the ancient Temple in Jerusalem.

A sprig of parsley dipped in salt water reminds Jews of
the tears their people shed when they were slaves.

Charoset, a paste of nuts, apples, and wine, reminds them
of the clay the slaves used to make bricks.

Bitter herbs recall the bitterness of slavery.

Matzoh, a flat bread, reminds them there was no time for
bread to rise before the slaves fled Egypt.

An egg symbolizes the new life that begins each spring.

Each year on the day of the spring equinox,

    ancient Saxons in Germany celebrated a festival

    for the goddess of springtime, named Eostre.

Her earthly symbol was a rabbit.

Rabbits and eggs were symbols of rebirth.

Many Anglo-Saxons in England dyed eggs

    by boiling them with flower petals and leaves.

Brightly colored eggs represented the bright sun

    of springtime.

At the same time that Pagans celebrated their goddess
of springtime, Eostre, Christians observed Jesus' new
beginning, when they believe he was raised from the dead.
As more people became Christians,
the name of their celebration changed from Eostre to Easter.

On the first Sunday

after the full moon after the spring equinox,

Christians celebrate Easter.

Many worship outdoors at early sunrise services

or in churches filled with flowers and glorious music.

Children find Easter baskets filled with chocolate rabbits

and colorful eggs, still symbols of Easter.

Today families of all kinds still celebrate spring
as a time of new beginnings.
They plant flowers and vegetables, play baseball, ride bikes,
fly kites, have picnics, enjoy the return of warm days,
and welcome spring, a new beginning.

Around June 21, the northern half of the world tilts toward the sun and the weather begins to warm. That's the Summer Solstice. Spring's over. Summer begins on the longest day of the year. On the same day in the southern half of the world, the earth tilts away from the sun and the Winter Solstice occurs. Fall's over. Winter begins on the shortest day of the year.

Around March 21, the sun is directly over the equator. In the northern half of the world that's the Spring Equinox. Winter's over. Spring begins.
On the same day in the southern half of the world, the Fall Equinox occurs. Summer's over. Fall begins.
All over the world there are 12 hours of day and 12 hours of night.

Around December 21, when the northern half of the world tilts away from the sun and the weather cools, that's the Winter Solstice. Fall's over. Winter begins on the shortest day of the year. On the same day, the southern half of the world tilts toward the sun and the Summer Solstice occurs. Spring's over. Summer begins on the longest day of the year.

Around September 21, the sun is directly over the equator. In the northern half of the world, that's the Fall Equinox. Summer's over. Fall begins.
On the same day in the southern half of the world, the Spring Equinox occurs. Winter's over. Spring begins.
All over the world there are 12 hours of day and 12 hours of night.

CHINESE NEW YEAR PAPER LANTERNS

The Chinese hold a Lantern Parade on the fifteenth night after the Chinese New Year. They put candles inside the lanterns, but your yellow paper will give your lantern a candlelike yellow glow. For another special effect, you can make a longer yellow cylinder and tape or glue several red shades to it. Make several paper lanterns and dangle them from long sticks.

What you need:

1 piece of heavy yellow paper (11"x 15")
1 piece of heavy red paper (12 "x 17 ")
tape or glue, scissors, pencil, a stick, string

What to do:

1. On the red paper, draw a line one inch from both long edges.
2. Fold the red paper in half so both long edges meet.
3. Make cuts about 1/2" apart on the folded part of the red paper down to the lines you have drawn—no farther.
4. Be careful. Don't cut through the unfolded edge.
5. Roll the heavy yellow paper lengthwise to make a long cylinder.
6. Tape or glue it together.
7. Open the red paper out.
8. Wrap the red paper lengthwise around the yellow cylinder.
9. Glue or tape the top and bottom of the red paper onto the cylinder.
10. Put the lantern on the stick with the string.

Have a lantern parade.

GROW NU RUZ SABZEH

Just as Iranian families have done for many years, you can grow *sabzeh*, a pot of wheat or barley. They plant the seeds two weeks before the first day of spring. On that day, the Spring Equinox, the Iranians welcome their New Year. They believe the sprouts symbolize new life and good fortune.

What you need:

a paper cup or bowl
rich potting soil
lentil or wheat seeds

What to do:

1. Fill the cup or bowl half full with soil.
2. Sprinkle seeds on top.
3. Cover the seeds with more soil.
4. Sprinkle with water.
5. Place the cup or bowl in a sunny window.
6. Water your mini-garden each day.
7. Watch the seeds sprout and grow.

DIANE'S MASHED POTATO EASTER EGGS

What you need:

2 cups of confectioners' (powdered) sugar
2 tablespoons soft butter
2 tablespoons cooled mashed potatoes
1 teaspoon vanilla
1/2 cup flaked coconut
melted chocolate
1 large mixing bowl
1 mixing spoon

What to do:

1. Mix the sugar, butter, potatoes, vanilla, and coconut.
2. Form into oval egg shapes.
3. Dip into melted chocolate.
4. Let them set for a few minutes for the chocolate to harden.

Share and enjoy!

MAKE CHAROSET, A TASTY TREAT

What you need:

1 cup of chopped apples

1 cup of chopped walnuts

1 teaspoon cinnamon

1 tablespoon red grape juice

What to do:

1. Mix apples, walnuts, cinnamon, and juice together.
2. Put in the refrigerator.

For something different:

Add cut-up dates, almonds, raisins, figs, and/or pecans.
With chopped Granny Smith green apples, add a bit of sugar.
Whatever combinations you use, enjoy your tasty treat.

CELEBRATE SPRING
MAKE A COLORFUL KITE

What you need:

*2 strong, straight dowels
   or bamboo sticks (90 cm and 102 cm)*
tape or glue
*1 sheet of plastic or cloth
   for the main part of the kite (102 cm square)*

heavy cord or twine
scissors
*Magic Markers, or paint,
   to decorate your kite*
about a dozen pieces of ribbon

What to do:

MAKING THE FRAME

1. Place the shorter stick across the larger stick to make a cross.
2. The two sticks should be at right angles to each other.
3. Glue them together.
4. Cut a notch at the ends of both sticks.
5. Cut the string long enough to go around the kite frame.
6. Make a loop in the top notch then wrap string around the stick.
7. Take the string through the notch at the crosspiece.
8. Make another loop at the bottom notch.
9. Slip the string through the notch at the other end of the crosspiece. Then up to the top.
10. Next, wrap the string a few times around the top.
11. Cut off any extra string.

PUTTING THE MATERIAL ON

1. Place the material down flat.
2. Put the stick frame on top, facedown.
3. Cut around the material. Leave extra to fold over the frame.
4. Tape or glue the material tightly around the frame.

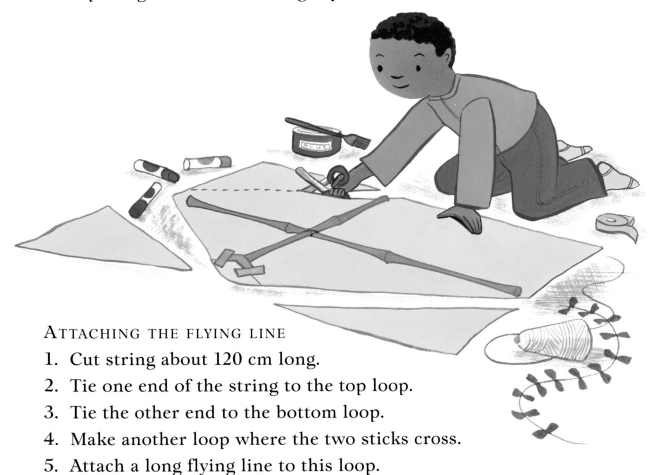

ATTACHING THE FLYING LINE

1. Cut string about 120 cm long.
2. Tie one end of the string to the top loop.
3. Tie the other end to the bottom loop.
4. Make another loop where the two sticks cross.
5. Attach a long flying line to this loop.
6. Tie the ribbons along a shorter piece of string to form the kite tail.
7. Attach this kite tail to the loop at the bottom.

Decorate your kite and let it soar.

FURTHER READING

Berger, Gilda. *Easter and Other Spring Holidays.* New York: Franklin Watts, 1983.

Epstein, Sam and Beryl. *A Holiday Book: European Folk Festivals.*
    Champaign, IL: Garrard Publishing Company, 1968.

Jackson, Ellen. *The Spring Equinox.* Brookfield, CT: The Millbrook Press, 2002.

James, E.O. *Seasonal Feasts and Festivals.* London: Thames and London, 1993.

Krishnaswami, Uma. *Holi.* New York: Children's Press, 2003.

MacMillan, Dianne. *Chinese New Year.* Hillside, NJ: Enslow Publishers, 1994.

Pfeffer, Wendy. *The Shortest Day: Celebrating the Winter Solstice.* New York: Dutton, 2003.

Pfeffer, Wendy. *We Gather Together: Celebrating the Fall Harvest.* New York: Dutton, 2006.

Simonds, Nina. *Moonbeams, Dumplings, and Dragon Boats.* New York: Gulliver Books, 2002.

WEBSITES

www.lost-civilizations.net/mayan-pyramids-chichen-itza.html
click on "Mayan Pyramids of Chichen Itza"

www.schooloftheseasons.com/spring.html

www.enchantedlearning.com/crafts/chinesenewyear/

www.world-mysteries.com/chichen_kukulcan.htm

www.internet-at-work.com/hos_mcgrane/holidays/olga.html

www.payvand.com/ny/massoume.html